K EEP ME CLEAN

REMEMBER TO WASH YOUR
HANDS BEFORE READING ME

D1318706

ELEPHANT BABY

Text adapted by Udiavar G. Rao
Illustrations by Robert Boehmer

Published by ENCYCLOPAEDIA BRITANNICA PRESS, Chicago,
and distributed in association with MEREDITH PRESS,
Des Moines and New York

The true-to-life photographs in this book are from the educational motion picture "Elephant Baby," produced for Encyclopaedia Britannica Films Inc. by Milan Herzog and photographed in the state of Mysore, India, by Peter Backhaus.

Elephants are not used for work as much as they used to be and they work only in places where machines cannot go. The photographer therefore had to seek them out in the jungle of Mysore, where he spent eighteen months living in the primitive conditions of a lumber camp.

Mr. U. G. Rao, who adapted the text of this book, is a native of Mysore and is now Publications Secretary of the India Association of Chicago.

The design of this book is by Ruth Rooney. Color reproduction was supervised by James Lockhart. The cover was designed by Don Walkoe.

The book has been carefully manufactured for long wear. The paper is 100-pound coated stock specially created for this series. The pages are side-sewn and are fixed into the case with sturdy end sheets. The laminated cover resists dirt and is washable.

The body type of this book is 18-point Kennerley Old Style, which was selected because its round character suggests the hero of the book.

INDIA

western

Mysore

Ghats

The state of Mysore in southern India is a hot, jungle region with dense forests on the mountain slopes and great rivers flowing through the valleys. Small villages cluster on the river banks. There are no roads or machines in parts of Mysore. For hauling and heavy work elephants are used.

Kalyani came slowly from the forest with her newborn baby.

"Kalyani! Kalyani!"

Raman was calling a mother elephant who had been let out into the forest to have her baby. Kalyani had lived wild in the jungle before she had been caught by Raman's father. Then she was tamed and taught to obey orders.

When Kalyani heard her name called, she came slowly toward Raman with her newborn baby.

The jungle growth was thick, and Kalyani guided her baby gently with her long trunk.

Raman smiled and hugged the new baby. "Cheria" he called him, which means "the little one."

Raman ordered Kalyani to kneel down, and he climbed onto her back. With his knees and toes he steered her toward the river. She moved slowly so that Cheria could keep up.

With her long trunk Kalyani gently guided her baby.

Cheria waded happily into the river and filled his trunk with water.

When they reached the river, Cheria waded happily in. Kalyani filled her trunk with several gallons of water and sprayed it over him. After Cheria had been thoroughly washed, Raman steered Kalyani home to show his family the new baby.

Raman had grown up with elephants. Whenever he was not in school, he liked to help care for his father's elephants. Raman's father was the *pancha,* or village chief, and was foreman of the forest lumber men. He owned five grown elephants.

Raman's family was happy to see Cheria, for he would add to their wealth when he grew big enough to work in the forest.

Drops of water sparkled on Cheria's baby hairs.

Raman chained Cheria's leg to a tree and tied a brass bell around his neck.

Raman's father brought a new brass bell for the baby. He told Raman to tie it on Cheria so that they would always be able to hear where he was. The baby elephant trumpeted and backed away when Raman tried to tie on the bell. So Raman chained Cheria's leg and tied the bell around his neck.

Tired out, Cheria flopped down to rest.

Although he was only a baby, Cheria was quite heavy. He weighed 230 pounds, about four times as much as Raman. But, like all very young creatures, he tired quickly and needed to rest. Suddenly he flopped down in the shade of one of the bamboo houses and slept.

The grown elephants went each day to work in the forest.

While Cheria was growing up, the grown elephants went each day to work in the forest.

The forest trees of Mysore are mostly teak, bamboo and sandalwood. Teak is very strong and is used for houses, ships and heavy furniture. Bamboo is used for making paper and for building in hot countries. Sandalwood gives fragrant oil and is also used for costly furniture and carvings.

Elephants work hard in the forest from dawn to dusk. Each elephant is guided by a *mahout*, its rider. With their powerful trunks elephants are able to uproot whole trees. With their strong white tusks they can lift the trees or drag them to a lumber camp. Here the villagers trim off the branches and saw the tree trunks by hand into large logs.

Then, with one end of a strong rope tied to each

Elephants can drag heavy logs through a jungle where no machines can go.

The elephants move fallen trees by pushing them with their heads.

log and the other end around an elephant's tusks, the elephants drag the logs to the river.

Teakwood is so hard that it cannot easily be sawed. So the teak logs are soaked in the river for a few days to soften them. When the logs are softer, the elephants pull them out of the water and drag them back to the lumber camp. This is hard work,

They lift huge logs with their tusks and trunk.

for the logs are now much heavier with water. But still the mighty elephants can move them. In the lumber camp the logs are sawed into thin planks.

Finally, the elephants carry the planks back to the river where they are lashed together and floated down the river to a big lumber yard. From here they are sent out to cities all over the world.

One elephant can do the work of forty strong men. A fully grown elephant is about nine feet high and weighs about 7000 pounds.

In spite of its great size, the elephant has quite small eyes. Its ears, however, are very large. They are also very tender, and the elephant moves them constantly to keep out insects. Even a tiny ant in the ear of an elephant is enough to drive the animal frantic.

The elephant's trunk is actually its nose and upper lip. The trunk has the strength to uproot a tree and yet the tip is so gentle that it can pick up a pea.

An elephant lives for about a hundred years. When it dies, an elephant is still useful, for its bones and valuable ivory tusks are used for various kinds of carvings.

The elephants drag the teak planks to the river.

Every evening the elephants went to the river to bathe.

Every evening, after the day's hard work, Raman's father led his elephants to the river to cool off. During the day their bodies got dirty, and the scorching sun baked the dirt in the creases of their skin. When the elephants soaked themselves, the dirt loosened. The daily bath also softened the tough skin and prevented it from cracking.

The elephants went deep into the river. They filled their trunks with water and sprayed it over their heads onto their bodies.

The tired elephants sank down into the cool water.

The *mahouts* helped to clean the tired elephants. They scrubbed the animals with handfuls of rough grass. Raman and other boys washed the elephants' bells at the edge of the river.

After they were well scrubbed, the elephants were led home. Raman's mother had cooked plenty of food for the hungry workers. A big mat was put before them and cooked rice, mixed with fruits, was spread on the mat. Raman and his family made balls of this mixture, which they fed to the elephants.

Elephants do not eat meat. They live on rice, bananas and other fruits, and tender leaves.

Cheria did not eat with the grown elephants.

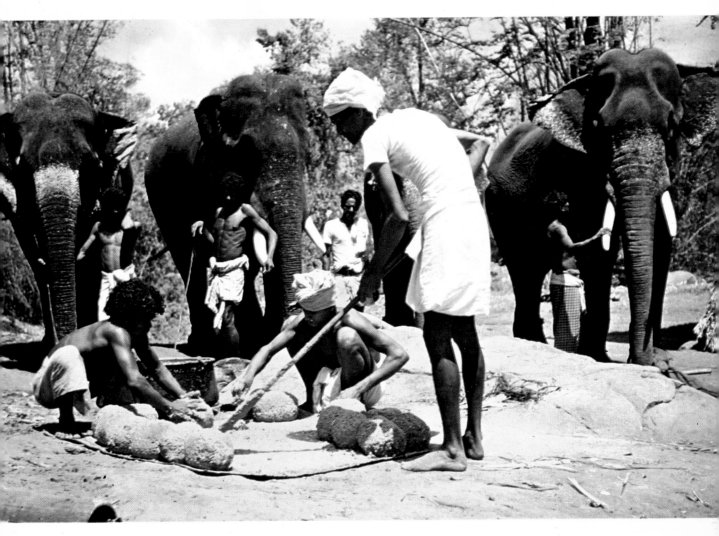

Raman and his family made balls of cooked rice for the elephants' meal.

He drank three gallons of his mother's milk each day. Elephant milk is the richest milk in the world.

After their meal the elephants were led to a bamboo stable. There they lay down to sleep on beds of hay and grass. The *mahouts* slept on cots nearby, keeping watch through the night.

Cheria spent his early years playing with Raman around the village and in the river. When he was five years old he was big enough to begin to work in the forest. But first he had to go to school.

Raman and Cheria played together in the river.

Raman's brother Gopal became his *mahout* and helped to train him. The "schoolroom" was a small pen made of strong bamboo poles and roofed with straw to keep out the hot sun.

Gopal tried to coax Cheria toward the pen.

Gopal pushed hard, but Cheria refused to budge.

Gopal and his father led Cheria toward the pen, but he refused to go in. Gopal pushed with all his strength, but Cheria would not budge. Even though he was still young, Cheria was very strong. At last an old, trained elephant had to be brought to push Cheria into the pen.

Cheria snorted and trumpeted at the heavy block of wood.

Inside the pen, Cheria trembled. He raised his trunk and trumpeted.

As his first lesson, Cheria had to learn to carry a rider, and Gopal was lowered onto his back.

The first few times Gopal was let down, the young elephant bucked wildly. Gopal was quickly pulled to safety.

After Cheria had got used to Gopal's weight, a block of teak-wood was lowered onto his back.

"*Irrkuka!*" shouted Gopal's father as the block forced Cheria down. This command meant that he was to kneel.

"*Ezhinelkuka!*" At this command the block was raised and Cheria could stand up. Cheria snorted and trumpeted at the heavy block of wood. He soon learned, however, that he got a banana when he obeyed commands and nothing when he did not.

Slowly Cheria grew to trust Gopal. He learned to kneel and to stay kneeling while Gopal climbed onto his back. He learned to stand up when told.

Cheria learned to trust Gopal and to carry him on his back.

Not until a mahout is sure that an elephant is well trained and trustworthy will he climb up its trunk and over its head, holding on to its big, fanlike ears.

It took time and patience to train the young elephant, but at last Cheria was ready to work with the other elephants. He learned to carry Gopal on his back and to walk in line behind the big elephants. He learned to uproot and move trees in the forest.

Cheria learned to follow the other elephants obediently.

Howdahs *were put on the backs of two big elephants to carry the hunters and their gear.*

Many fierce animals—bears, tigers and leopards—live in the dense forests of Mysore. They are often a danger, killing livestock and sometimes even people.

Not long after Cheria was trained, he went on his first tiger hunt. One of the villagers reported that a tiger had killed his dog and terrified his family. Another told of hearing wild screams in the jungle. So Gopal's father, as village *pancha,* organized a hunt.

He ordered *howdahs*—large saddles—to be put on the backs of two huge elephants. The *howdahs* carried the hunters and their gear. Gopal's father himself rode Cheria.

A band of villagers went out with drums and trumpets. They made a great noise in the jungle, trying to drive the tiger toward the hunters. The hunters waited nervously as the noise of the villagers came closer and closer. Suddenly the tiger burst from some bushes right in front of Cheria!

The villagers made a great noise to drive the tiger toward the hunters.

Gopal's father raised his gun. Cheria stiffened. The tiger sprang, and Gopal's father fired! Before the

The dead tiger was tied to two strong poles and carried to the village.

tiger reached Cheria, it fell to the ground. The bullet had hit it in the head.

The dead tiger was tied to two poles. It took four men to carry the heavy body to the village.

The colorful skin was removed and hung up in the *pancha*'s house as a trophy of the hunt.

The villagers came to admire the skin and to join Gopal's family in a feast celebrating the success of the tiger hunt.

Cheria was rewarded with a feast of bananas.

Cheria had proved himself obedient, even in great danger. Gopal and his father were proud of him and rewarded him with a feast of bananas.

"Cheria behaved well today," said Gopal's father. "He will be a good worker."

"A great hunter, too," said Gopal. "But we must not call him Cheria any more. He's 'Omban Yanai' now."

And so Cheria, "the little one," became Omban Yanai, "the grown elephant," and took his place among the adult elephants.

Date Due